COMMON
BIRDS
of the South-West Forests

by Carolyn Thomson-Dans and John Hunter

GOVERNMENT OF WESTERN AUSTRALIA

DEPARTMENT OF
Conservation
AND LAND MANAGEMENT
Conserving the nature of WA

INTRODUCTION

Birds are a very visible and attractive component of the wildlife of the south-west forests. Whether you glimpse a flash of vibrant blue, courtesy of one of the local splendid fairy-wrens, as you drive or walk down a forest track, or spot the majestic wedge-tailed eagle on the wing, our birds have enormous capacity to delight and entertain. Forest birds are exceptionally diverse, ranging from the emu, which is the second largest bird in the world, to the dainty little robins.

Forest birds have many different lifestyles. Some, such as parrots, usually live high in the canopy, where they exploit eucalypt and other blossoms and thereby play an important role in pollinating tall forest trees. Mistletoebirds have become specialised at eating the berries of mistletoe, a semi-parasitic plant that grows in the canopy of many forest trees, and subsequently distributing and fertilising the seeds when it excretes. The pallid cuckoo, on the other hand, begins its life by ejecting the eggs and young of its adopted parents. While emus peck for seed and vegetable matter on the forest floor, rufous treecreepers search for ants on tree trunks and fallen logs. Western yellow robins perch low down on trunks and branches and drop onto insects in the leaf litter, grey fantails sally for insects from an exposed perch and striated pardalotes glean sap-sucking insects from leaves high in the canopy.

Many forest birds are not only strikingly beautiful but readily discovered on a short drive from Perth. This book covers a selection of some of the most common birds that you will encounter when travelling through the south-west forests. The area covered is between Perth, Augusta and Albany, but many of the species that have been described are also found elsewhere.

Habitat and food keys are provided for each species, with the appropriate symbols highlighted.

HABITAT

forest

woodland

low woodland

heath

FOOD

seeds

fruits

flowers

small animals

insects

EMU
(Dromaius novaehollandiae)

The emu is Australia's largest native bird, and the second largest flightless bird in the world. The birds were once a favoured food of Aboriginal people, who would sometimes place poison plants in waterholes to drug their prey, or attract the birds by imitating their calls. In agricultural areas they are regarded as a pest, as they can damage fences and watering points and compete with stock for food and water. In 1932, WA farmers even declared an emu war, calling in an army detachment with two Lewis (machine) guns to exterminate them. They have been farmed for their valuable meat, skins and feathers for some years.

DESCRIPTION: This large bird grows up to two metres high. Its back is decorated with soft, brownish-grey feathers and it has long, powerful legs. Each large foot has three toes.

STATUS AND DISTRIBUTION: Emus are common and found throughout the Australian mainland. They are now absent from built-up areas, such as Perth and its suburbs.

PREFERRED HABITAT: They live in a wide range of habitats including deserts, dense coastal shrublands, eucalypt woodlands and forests.

LIFE HISTORY: Emus dine on native fruits, vegetation and ground-dwelling insects. Adult birds are usually found in pairs or small parties. They are highly nomadic and in the breeding season they move into areas of recent good rains. Breeding is usually from March to November, when a sparse nest of grass, bark and sticks is built on the ground. The father does all the parenting. He broods between five and 11 dark green eggs. The male also escorts the chicks, which have attractive black and yellow stripes. At about 18 months the large juveniles disperse.

Above: *Male emu with chicks*   Below: *Emu footprints and scats*

CALL: The females make an unusual drumming sound, but both sexes make deep grunts.

BROWN GOSHAWK

(Accipiter fasciatus)

Brown goshawks prey on a variety of birds, mammals, frogs and reptiles, usually taking them completely by surprise. Their liking for the young of domestic "chooks" has earned them the name of "chickenhawk".

DESCRIPTION: Females are larger than males; they are between 47 and 56 centimetres long, compared with the 40 to 43 centimetre males (though northern forms of this species are considerably smaller). The wings and back of this bird are deep brown, with a more rufous collar. The tail is brown, with darker brown barring, and the breast and underparts are beautifully patterned with chestnut and cream barring, which must offer these stealth hunters superb camouflage. The eyes are a piercing yellow.

OTHER NAMES: Chickenhawk, Australian goshawk.

STATUS AND DISTRIBUTION: Brown goshawks range across most of Australia, with the exception of a few central areas, and extend to Tasmania, New Guinea and other Pacific islands.

PREFERRED HABITAT: They are common in eucalypt forests and woodlands and inland watercourses lined with trees, avoiding areas with no cover. They are also well represented in urban areas.

LIFE HISTORY: Both partners build their nest of sticks with great care, taking up to four weeks to do so. The nest is large and placed in the horizontal fork of a tree, high off the ground. The female does most of the incubation, after laying from one to five eggs at intervals of between two and four days, while the male brings food to the nest for mother and chicks.

CALL: Brown goshawks are usually silent, but do make a variety of sounds when excited or disturbed.

WEDGE-TAILED EAGLE

(Aquila audax)

The wedge-tailed eagle is awe-inspiring, with its huge size, powerful wings and hooked bill. This majestic bird has a massive wingspan of up to two and a half metres. One of the most-maligned birds of prey, it was persecuted for decades because of the misapprehension that it destroyed livestock. Australia's largest bird of prey now enjoys full protection. The birds are usually seen soaring over paddocks and woodlands in country areas.

DESCRIPTION: Wedge-tailed eagles have large legs and feet with deadly talons. Many birds are blackish-brown to nearly black, while others are a pale brown with creamy buff highlights. Young birds are light in colour; the darker the bird the older it is. Seen from below, the tail is long and distinctively wedge-shaped.

OTHER NAMES: Eagle-hawk, wedgie.

STATUS AND DISTRIBUTION: Wedge-tailed eagles are still moderately common and found in all parts of Australia.

PREFERRED HABITAT: These birds inhabit forests, open country and mountain ranges.

LIFE HISTORY: Depending on the landscape, the species nests in a variety of sites: in a low dead tree in a desert, a prominent tree top on a hillside, on the ground on an island, but always far away from human habitation. The nest is a large platform of sticks. There are normally two eggs but often only one chick survives. Immature eagles move out of breeders' territories, some moving to the coastal plains where they are often surprised in groups, squabbling over road kills. They hunt rabbits, small kangaroos and wallabies, and sometimes birds and reptiles.

CALL: These birds may make a variety of calls, such as a cat-like screech or repeated double whistle.

Photo - Jiri Lochman/Lochman Transparencies

RED-TAILED BLACK-COCKATOO

(Calyptorhynchus banksii)

Large and noisy red-tailed black-cockatoos are among the most spectacular Australian birds. However, in the tall jarrah and karri forests they usually stay high up in the canopy, where they feast on marri and other eucalypt seeds. They extract the nutritious seeds of marri by tearing open the base of the fruits. They also form smaller groups than in other areas, usually pairs or small family parties.

DESCRIPTION: These birds have a prominent crest above their strong grey bills. Male cockatoos are uniformly black, with a brilliant crimson band on the tail feathers. The females are brownish-black, with yellow speckles and light yellow to orange tail bands. Adult birds are between 50 and 61 centimetres long.

STATUS AND DISTRIBUTION: In WA, red-tailed black-cockatoos are on a reserve list of species whose status requires monitoring and review. Their nests are sometimes robbed by illegal wildlife traffickers and their habitat has been considerably reduced by clearing.

PREFERRED HABITAT: They require nesting hollows with an entrance at least 180 millimetres wide. In the karri forest these can be 30 metres from the ground.

LIFE HISTORY: Red-tailed black-cockatoos lay one, sometimes two eggs, in a nesting hollow lined with wood dust and chips, usually high above the ground. They enter the hollow tail first. Regardless of the number of eggs, only one young is reared. The male feeds his partner while she sits on the eggs and broods the nestlings. In the south-west, these birds lay their eggs between March and April and from July to October.

CALL: The call is a harsh "kree".

BAUDIN'S BLACK-COCKATOO
(*Calyptorhynchus baudinii*)

Baudin's black-cockatoos greatly resemble Carnaby's black cockatoos but differ in their food, their habitat and their slightly larger bill. In fact, it was only recently realised that they were two separate species. They extract the seeds of marri—their favourite food—by biting off the capsule and holding it by the left foot, pulling out the seeds with the extended tip of the bill. They also feed on bull banksia seeds, nectar, wood-boring larvae and may raid orchards to remove the seeds from fruit. After bushfires, they may feast on seeds shed en masse by burnt trees.

DESCRIPTION: Baudin's black-cockatoos are up to 60 centimetres long. These large birds have very long tails with a broad white band. Their dusky black feathers have an off-white edge, creating a pattern of thin crescents which is most obvious on the breast. The bill has a long tip and there is a white cheek patch.

OTHER NAMES: Long-billed or white-tailed black-cockatoo.

STATUS AND DISTRIBUTION: These birds are given special protection under WA's Wildlife Conservation Act. Because the species is very long-lived their decline in numbers may not be obvious, but young birds are particularly uncommon. Baudin's black-cockatoos are found from the Darling Range near Perth to the Stirling Range on the South Coast.

PREFERRED HABITAT: They live largely in WA's karri forests.

LIFE HISTORY: Baudin's black-cockatoos form permanent pairs. They lay two eggs in a large hollow high up in a jarrah, marri or karri tree. Only one chick usually survives. After breeding, they flock together and fly north to the Darling Range or east to forested parts of the Stirling Range.

CALL: They make wailing cries when in flight.

Photo - Jiri Lochman/Lochman Transparencies

PURPLE-CROWNED LORIKEET

(*Glossopsitta porphyrocephala*)

Eucalypt blossoms attract these colourful lorikeets, which feed on pollen, nectar, the blossoms themselves, and occasionally insects and larvae. Purple-crowned lorikeets have a crimson patch under each pointed wing, which can be seen as they fly overhead.

DESCRIPTION: These striking birds have an orange forehead, a red patch in front of the eyes and a dark purple crown. The rest of the back, wings and upper tail is largely bright green, except for an oval patch of orange yellow behind the eyes and the brilliant turquoise on the curve of the wings. The throat, breast and belly are a pale blue. The underside of the tail is yellow and green.

OTHER NAMES: Porphry-crowned lorikeet, zit parrot.

STATUS AND DISTRIBUTION: Purple-crowned lorikeets range from about Geraldton through the south-west and along the entire southern coast of Australia. They are nomadic, appearing in areas of abundant blossom and can be seasonally common.

PREFERRED HABITAT: They favour eucalypt woodlands with suitable hollows for nesting. These include WA's mallee and wandoo woodlands and the dense karri forests of the south-west.

LIFE HISTORY: Purple-crowned lorikeets may feed and nest in flocks. Each female lays three to four eggs in a suitable tree hollow, usually within a eucalypt near water. The female does most of the incubation, while the male brings her food, though she does leave the nest for short periods to feed on her own.

CALL: These noisy birds make a constant high "tsi-i-it" in flight and a shrill twittering while feeding.

RED-CAPPED PARROT

(Purpureicephalus spurius)

This species is one of Australia's most beautiful parrots. Red-capped parrots chew the soft, immature "honkey nuts" of the marri to extract the seeds, and they prefer the hollows of marri for nesting. In fact, the distribution of this bird largely coincides with that of its favourite nesting and food tree. Although they usually feed high in the canopy, red-capped parrots do descend to the ground to consume grass seeds, so that flashes of exotic colours are sometimes seen along grassy roadsides.

DESCRIPTION: These medium-sized birds are about 36 centimetres long. The males have a scarlet crown, a broad yellow band around the neck, purple breast, red rump and bright green wings and back, with blue flight feathers. The tail is an even richer green, edged with bright blue. The females and immature males are duller and have larger areas of green.

OTHER NAMES: King parrot, pileated parakeet, hookbill.

STATUS AND DISTRIBUTION: Red-capped parrots are found only in WA, from Dandaragan, north of Perth, to just west of Esperance, but are common in areas of suitable habitat within this range.

PREFERRED HABITAT: They favour eucalypt forests and woodlands.

LIFE HISTORY: Immature birds form wandering bands of 20 or so and are seen more frequently than the adults, which pair off and settle down to a defined patch of the forest. They nest in hollows high above the ground, laying around five eggs in each clutch. The female incubates the young, which vacate the nest about five weeks after hatching.

CALL: They "kurr-ak" repeatedly during flight and shriek when alarmed.

WESTERN ROSELLA

(Platycercus icterotis)

Despite being brightly coloured, western rosellas tend to be quiet and unobtrusive. These birds stay near cover, usually only moving short distances at a time, flying swiftly from one tree to another.

DESCRIPTION: Male western rosellas have crimson heads and underparts, apart from their pale yellow cheeks. The back feathers are black with red and dark green edges, but the flight feathers are cobalt blue. The long, tapering tail is largely blue, mixed with white, green and black. They are smaller than most other rosellas, only about 26 centimetres from head to tail. The females are much duller than males.

OTHER NAMES: Yellow-cheeked rosella, Stanley rosella.

STATUS AND DISTRIBUTION: They are found only in the south-western corner of WA, from Moora to Dundas. Although they are common in parts of their range, they are becoming scarce in parts of the Wheatbelt.

PREFERRED HABITAT: These birds inhabit forests, woodlands and other areas. They are often seen in paddocks that have been recently harvested, picking up fallen grain.

LIFE HISTORY: Western rosellas readily consume seeds, berries, nuts, fruits, blossoms, nectar and insects, including larvae. They mate for life and nest in eucalypt hollows, where they lay between three and seven eggs. They rarely form flocks but family groups may forage together in areas where food is plentiful.

CALL: They make a soft and musical sound made up of repeated two-note whistles.

PALLID CUCKOO
(Cuculus pallidus)

The pallid cuckoo is probably better known as the rain bird, or weather bird. It is instantly recognised by its unique call, which is usually uttered by the male during the breeding season.

DESCRIPTION: Adult birds are slim and about 30 centimetres long. The male has a plain brownish-grey back and pale grey underparts and a long grey tail which is notched with white. The female is much more spotted above and is tinged with chestnut and buff on the head and tail. They have a large white spot on the nape of the neck.

STATUS AND DISTRIBUTION: The pallid cuckoo is common but numbers fluctuate notably. Seen alone or in pairs and trios, this migratory bird arrives in the south-west of WA from May to July and leaves in December.

HABITAT: The species is found in woodlands, parks, paddocks, on road verges, in well-treed urban areas and scrubby areas.

LIFE HISTORY: The pallid cuckoo often feeds on hairy caterpillars. This parasitic species lays its eggs in the open nests of other bush birds, such as honeyeaters. The cuckoo chick usually survives at the expense of the host's offspring and is looked after by its adopted parents. It will eventually fly away and repeat the saga.

CALL: The song of the male cuckoo consists of a series of notes ascending in scale, a staccato "pip-pip-pip-pip-pip-pip-pip-pip", with the second note lower than the first. The female emits a brassy whistle.

TAWNY FROGMOUTH

(Podargus strigoides)

When it roosts, the tawny frogmouth looks just like a broken branch, closing its eyes to slits and remaining frozen, even when disturbed. The birds are a quite remarkable sight, especially when roosting close together in family groups of two or more.

DESCRIPTION: Tawny frogmouths derive their common name from their distinctive large wide bills. These birds are the same silvery grey colour as dead, weathered wood, with black camouflaging streaks and occasional brown and white flecks. They are between 35 and 53 centimetres long, with the females only slightly smaller than the males.

OTHER NAMES: Podargus.

STATUS AND DISTRIBUTION: These birds are common and found in all parts of Australia, including Tasmania and some offshore islands.

PREFERRED HABITAT: Tawny frogmouths inhabit open forests and woodlands of eucalypts and acacias.

LIFE HISTORY: These birds hunt by night, taking large nocturnal invertebrates such as spiders and centipedes. They are creatures of habit, staying in the same patch of woodland year after year and using the same roosts and nesting sites. Their home range is about 20 to 80 hectares. Both parents participate in nest-building, incubation, brooding and capturing food during nesting. One to three eggs are laid in a flimsy platform of twigs on horizontal branches or sometimes stumps.

CALL: Tawny frogmouths advertise their nest sites with a drumming noise, an "ooom, ooom, ooom", repeated in bursts of between 10 and 50. A rattling noise and other sounds are also made.

SCARLET ROBIN

(Petroica multicolor)

During courtship, a male scarlet robin will feed a female, to convince her of his credentials as a mate, then extend each wing downwards to show off his alluring white wing patches.

DESCRIPTION: Males have a bright red breast, and a black chin, head, back and tail. There is a large white patch above the beak and a broad white patch on each wing. The undertail and rump are also white. Females are much paler, with a greyish-brown throat, back, wings and tail. There are, however, white feathers on the wings and tail. The breast is a duller red with a white belly and undertail. Adults are between 12 and 13 centimetres long.

OTHER NAMES: Scarlet-breasted robin, white-capped robin.

STATUS AND DISTRIBUTION: These birds are common in south-western and south-eastern Australia and Tasmania.

PREFERRED HABITAT: They inhabit eucalypt forests and woodlands with a scrubby understorey.

LIFE HISTORY: Scarlet robins are territorial birds. Females build a neat, fibrous nest, usually camouflaged with bark, while the male perches and sings nearby. He does, however, feed his mate while she is sitting on about three eggs and he also helps to feed the nestlings. The birds feed by snatching insects on the wing or extracting them from leaves or bark.

CALL: The male produces a short, rippling song of "wee-cheedalee-dalee".

Above: *Male scarlet robin at nest*   Below: *The female*

WHITE-BREASTED ROBIN

(Eopsaltria georgiana)

Dainty white-breasted robins typically perch sideways on a tree trunk, waiting for insects to stray near them. Then they dive out to pluck beetles, wasps, ants and other prey from the ground or the air.

DESCRIPTION: These small birds are only about 15 centimetres long. They have a grey head and upper back and darker grey wing and tail feathers. The breast and other underparts are white. In flight, a white bar is visible through the base of the tail feathers.

OTHER NAMES: White-bellied robin.

STATUS AND DISTRIBUTION: These birds are confined to southwestern Australia, ranging from just north of Geraldton to Esperance in areas reasonably close to the coast.

PREFERRED HABITAT: White-breasted robins are particularly common in the karri forest. They inhabit dense thickets along streams, within forests or in coastal heaths.

LIFE HISTORY: During courtship, the male will feed the female. White-breasted robins lay about two eggs in a cup-like nest in the fork of a small tree. There is an extended family that includes the offspring from previous years. These birds help to catch food for the brooding mother and her nestlings. Together, they may raise three broods in the one season. They will bravely feign a broken wing to distract intruders from a nearby nest.

CALL: The male produces a chirruping song and a variety of other calls are made by both sexes, including a "twick-twick". They will "chirr" when alarmed.

WESTERN YELLOW ROBIN

(Eopsaltria griseogularis)

Western yellow robins make short forays from nearby branches and tree trunks to pluck up invertebrates such as ants, spiders, larvae, beetles, wasps and small cockroaches. These are taken mostly from the ground.

DESCRIPTION: These small (about 15 centimetre long) birds are silvery grey, with a white throat and bright yellow rump. They have a short bill and spindly black legs. Males and females have the same plumage.

OTHER NAMES: Grey-breasted robin.

STATUS AND DISTRIBUTION: These birds are reasonably common across the south-western corner of the State and a small area in South Australia. They are distributed as far north as Shark Bay. However, their range and numbers have substantially declined as a result of clearing.

PREFERRED HABITAT: Western yellow robins live in eucalypt forests, open woodlands and mallee. They prefer areas with scrubby undergrowth for cover.

LIFE HISTORY: They build well-camouflaged, cup-like nests in the forks of living or dead trees, in which two eggs are usually laid. The female attends to incubation and brooding, while her partner collects food for her and the chicks. Other birds may also help collect food. Robins often feign injury, painfully trailing a "broken" wing along the ground if an intruder comes too close to the nestlings. When not breeding they sometimes form small flocks.

CALL: Western yellow robins produce a series of trilled whistles at dawn. At other times they repeat plaintive soft piping notes at the same pitch.

GOLDEN WHISTLER

(Pachycephala pectoralis)

One of the typical birds of the south-west forests, golden whistlers glean most of their prey from trees, but sometimes swoop out to take insects on the wing or to rifle through the litter on the forest floor. The loud song rings out noisily throughout the breeding season.

DESCRIPTION: Only the mature male birds have brightly coloured plumage. They have a black head, face and beak with a white throat. The back of the head and chest are a bright yellow, the tail and wing feathers are dusky black to grey and the back is a yellowish-green. The females are a dull greyish-green.

OTHER NAMES: White-throated whistler, golden-breasted thickhead.

STATUS AND DISTRIBUTION: These birds are common in the south-west of WA, from Shark Bay to Esperance. They are also found in parts of eastern Australia.

PREFERRED HABITAT: Golden whistlers seem to prefer taller, wetter coastal forests but they are also found in eucalypt woodlands, heath and mallee areas.

LIFE HISTORY: Golden whistlers generally eat insects and their larvae. The nest is untidy and shaped like a cup. They lay two eggs between September and January and both parents incubate the eggs and care for their young.

CALL: While breeding, these birds make a loud whistling "chee-chee-chee-chee-tu-whit".

GREY FANTAIL
(Rhipidura fuliginosa)

These small birds are hyperactive; twisting, turning, fluttering, spiralling and zigzagging gracefully through the boughs and foliage of the forest. As well as earning them the alternative common name of "mad fan", these aerial feats enable them to snap up meals of flying insects from mid-air.

DESCRIPTION: Grey fantails are about 16 centimetres long and grey over their upper bodies. Some of the wing and tail feathers are, however, edged with white. They have a white brow and a thin white stripe behind each eye, as well as a white throat. The rest of the underparts are creamy buff. The tail is, of course, fan-shaped.

OTHER NAMES: White-shafted fantail, mad fan.

STATUS AND DISTRIBUTION: These birds are common and found across the entire Australian mainland, as well as Tasmania.

PREFERRED HABITAT: They inhabit all types of forests and woodlands.

LIFE HISTORY: Grey fantails lay between two and four eggs in a distinctive but tiny cup-like nest. This has a tail up to 15 millimetres long hanging beneath it and is bound neatly with cobwebs. These are built in the fork of a tree. They may forage alone or in loose groups.

CALL: They produce a high upward climbing song with eight to 10 notes and call to each other with a single or double "chip".

SPLENDID FAIRY-WREN

(*Malurus splendens*)

Out of the breeding season, you may barely notice male splendid wrens, but in their courting plumage they are among the most striking birds of the forest. With their iridescent cobalt blue feathers, these little birds certainly are splendid.

DESCRIPTION: Breeding males are almost completely bright blue, with a lighter cheek patch and black bands across the eye, nape and breast. The wings are blackish-blue, with a greenish metallic sheen. Non-breeding males are a drabber greyish-brown, but with bluish wings and a white-tipped blue tail. Their undersides are dull white. Females are similar, but have greyish-brown wings, less colourful tails and a rufous tinge around their eyes and neck. They are about 12 centimetres long.

OTHER NAMES: Banded wren, turquoise wren.

STATUS AND DISTRIBUTION: Splendid fairy-wrens are reasonably common, although they have largely disappeared from cleared areas. They are found across most of the southern half of Australia, except for the Nullarbor Plain and closely settled areas.

PREFERRED HABITAT: These birds inhabit jarrah forests, woodlands, mulga and mallee areas.

LIFE HISTORY: Splendid fairy-wrens are territorial birds that tend to stay in one place for most of their lives. They live in small groups, with all the members defending the territory and feeding the young. As a result, the breeding female, who does all nest building and brooding, is able to raise several broods. Between two and four eggs are laid at a time, in a loose oval-shaped nest of grass, usually from September to January.

CALL: The song is a loud, rich warbling. Several shorter calls, such as a staccato "prip-prip", are also made.

RED-WINGED FAIRY-WREN
(*Malurus elegans*)

The red-winged fairy-wren is easily distinguished by the beautiful chestnut plumage of its shoulders, the light blue capping on its head and its contrasting dark blue throat. It likes the wettest areas of forests, such as moist gullies and thickly vegetated creeklines.

DESCRIPTION: Apart from the colouring described above, the males have greyish-brown wings and a greyish-white belly. The females and non-breeding males are greyish-brown above, with a white breast and throat. The long elegant dusky blue tail is usually held high above the bird's back.

OTHER NAMES: Elegant fairy-wren, marsh wren.

STATUS AND DISTRIBUTION: The red-winged fairy-wren is restricted to the south-western corner of WA.

PREFERRED HABITAT: This bird typically inhabits dense scrub such as thickly vegetated gullies and vegetation along creeklines.

LIFE HISTORY: Red-winged fairy-wrens are largely insect eaters, but will also take seeds. They are social and live in small, close-knit groups of up to five birds. As well as building the nest in which she deposits two or three eggs between September to December, the breeding female does all of the incubation herself. However, other members of the group may help to collect food for both her and the young.

CALL: This species makes a soft "treee". The song is a high-pitched warbling, with some introductory chirps.

Above: *Male red-winged fairy-wren*   Below: *The female*

WHITE-BROWED SCRUBWREN

(Sericornis frontalis)

The WA form of the white-browed scrubwren differs from those found in the east by the distinctive black spots found on its throat and breast.

DESCRIPTION: The upper body of this small (11 to 14 centimetre) bird is olive brown to reddish-brown, with a darker head and lighter rump. There is a distinctive white brow above the eye and a white line below the eye. The throat and breast are covered with black spots. The tail is tipped with white.

OTHER NAMES: Spotted scrubwren, buff-breasted scrubwren.

STATUS AND DISTRIBUTION: These birds are found from Shark Bay, around the southern and eastern coasts of Australia to Queensland. They also live in Tasmania.

PREFERRED HABITAT: White-browed scrubwrens inhabit moist, densely vegetated areas.

LIFE HISTORY: These birds construct a coarse dome of bark, roots and grasses. This is cleverly hidden under bark, between tree trunks or in a tangle of vegetation. White-browed scrubwrens produce two or three eggs. Family groups are often formed and they forage together and help the breeding pair to feed the nestlings.

CALL: "Churrs" and "chips" are used to communicate and they produce a whistled song.

WESTERN GERYGONE

(Gerygone fusca)

The western gerygone is one of the fairy warblers that are well known as fine-billed, charming and for having a distinctive song.

DESCRIPTION: Only about 10 centimetres long, the bird is a cinnamon brownish-grey with an indistinct white eyebrow and whitish underparts. There is a band of white at the base of the tail. The male and female are alike.

OTHER NAMES: Western warbler or white-tailed warbler.

STATUS AND DISTRIBUTION: This species is the only gerygone to range around Australia in three separate areas; east, central and west. It is a common bird in the south-west of WA, and the population seems to migrate to northern areas in the Gascoyne and Pilbara in winter.

PREFERRED HABITAT: In WA, the western gerygone occupies coastal eucalypt forests and woodlands of the south-west, mallee in the east and mulga woodlands in the centre.

LIFE HISTORY: The bird gathers small insects from the outer foliage of trees, usually high above the ground. It can sometimes be seen taking insects on the wing, as it hovers above the crown of a tree. In the breeding season, the male signals his territory by singing. While the female builds a nest, the male sits nearby; singing, bowing, fanning his tail and flicking his wings. Normal movements give the impression of restlessness, and the bird frequently shakes itself. The hooded nest of vegetable matter, cobwebs and grass stems is often parasitised by cuckoos.

CALL: When feeding together a pair will occasionally chatter softly. The male song has a sweet, soft and slow group of notes which rise fast then fall away to finish prematurely.

41

INLAND THORNBILL

(Acanthiza apicalis)

This endlessly active small brownish bird ranges across most of southern Australia and inland. Up to 10 subspecies are thought to exist.

DESCRIPTION: Males and females are similar in colour, the upper parts being a rich olive brown, to brownish-grey. In the grey form, the rump is more rufous brown, the wings darker greyish-brown, with paler edges, and the tail is a dark greyish-brown with a black band. The face has olive to pale grey flecks, and the forehead has russet to white scalloping. The underparts are cream to pure white, grading to olive brown. The throat and breast are clearly streaked greyish-black and the eye is red.

STATUS AND DISTRIBUTION: Inland thornbills are found throughout the southern Australian mainland. They also live in Tasmania and on offshore islands. These birds are common, except in the drier parts of their range.

PREFERRED HABITAT: The species favours a variety of habitats, from dense eucalypt forest to arid mulga woodlands. It is also found in waterway and dune vegetation and often occurs in pockets of dense scrub, between one and five metres high.

LIFE HISTORY: Mornings and afternoons are usually spent foraging through foliage, gleaning insects from the branches and leaves of one bush before checking out the next. Insects are taken from various flowering plants, hence they are often seen working up the "spikes" of blackboys. Inland thornbills mix with the feeding flocks of other birds, except during the breeding season. The female builds the nest and incubates the eggs, while the male sings in defence of the territory.

CALL: The song is a series of whistled twitters which end in a metallic trill. The call is a soft whistling and chipping. When pestered by cuckoos, brown thornbills produce a harsh churring sound. Mimicry is often used.

WESTERN THORNBILL

(Acanthiza inornata)

Western thornbills spend their days procuring beetles, bugs and other insects from the undergrowth, usually in groups of up to a dozen. When not breeding, they may move reasonable distances, often in association with other insect-eating birds. They have the dullest colouring of all the thornbills.

DESCRIPTION: Western thornbills are a plain olive grey above and creamy buff below. The face and forehead have a yellowish tinge and are slightly mottled. The birds are small, between nine and 10 centimetres long when fully grown.

OTHER NAMES: Bark-tit.

STATUS AND DISTRIBUTION: These birds are common and occur across the south-western corner of the State.

PREFERRED HABITAT: They live in woodlands, open forests with undergrowth and heath.

LIFE HISTORY: Western thornbills breed from August to December. They usually deposit four eggs into a dome-shaped nest. The nest, made from grass and strips of bark, is concealed close to the ground.

CALL: The song is produced in rapid staccato bursts.

YELLOW-RUMPED THORNBILL

(Acanthiza chrysorrhoa)

The yellow-rumped thornbill is known locally to "old-timers" as the tomtit and is one of the most widespread of the thornbills. Their nests are bulky constructions with a "false nest" or cup at the top and a concealed side entrance.

DESCRIPTION: The feature that best distinguishes this bird from other thornbills is its bright yellow rump. Both sexes are similar in colour and markings. Between 10 to 12 centimetres long, the birds are perhaps the largest and the most distinctly marked of the thornbills. They have a bright yellow rump, a white eyebrow, white spotted black crown and pale eyes.

STATUS AND DISTRIBUTION: In WA the birds are common from the Ashburton River, through the upper Gascoyne and Murchison Rivers and south-east to the Great Australian Bight.

PREFERRED HABITAT: The birds are found in open woodlands, forest clearings, scrublands, grasslands, paddocks and garden shrubbery.

LIFE HISTORY: Yellow-rumped thornbills spend most of their time in "edge" habitat, using the bush for roosting and nesting and the clearings of bare ground for foraging. The birds work in loose lines, foraging for insects, spiders, caterpillars and occasional seeds with jerky hops. They are both sedentary and communal and out of breeding they gather in groups of up to 30 in a clan territory. They break into smaller groups to breed, with several males to each female.

CALL: The song is a descending bright and merry tinkerling, repeated two or three times in cycles. The contact call in flight is a sharp repeated "check", while softer chips and a subsong are common among the group.

VARIED SITTELLA

(*Daphoenositta chrysoptera*)

These small birds are noted for their engaging behaviour; they often hang upside down or climb head first down tree trunks.

DESCRIPTION: There are five races of the varied sittella, ranging in colour from a grey bird with a white head, to a bird with a black cap, cinnamon wings, a black tail and white underparts. Other variations include orange wings, white wings and striated colouring. The beak is slightly upturned and they have quite large feet, large wings and short tails. The slightly larger black-capped sittella is the usual form found in southern WA.

STATUS AND DISTRIBUTION: Varied sittellas are found throughout most of mainland Australia.

PREFERRED HABITAT: They inhabit eucalypt woodlands and open forests, as well as mallee and acacia woodlands, orchards, parks and scrubby gardens.

LIFE HISTORY: The varied sittella lives solely among the trees, where it forages in small parties. After looking for spiders, beetles, caterpillars, bees and bugs in one tree, the whole group floats and dips to the next. If frightened, they hide in cracks or hang upside down like motionless leaves. They often climb down tree trunks inspecting bark, flicking their wings to disturb prey. Captures are usually held by one foot and stabbed with the beak. The birds roost in groups and preen each other while perched. Nest building is also a communal effort resulting in a superb nest which is camouflaged with bark from the supporting tree trunk.

CALL: The usual call is a thin, high-pitched "seewit-seewee" in flight. Flocks also give a continual "chip-chip". The alarm call is best described as "didididit" and the song "tzir, zit-zit, tzir-zit-zat-zat".

RUFOUS WHISTLER

(*Pachycephala rufiventris*)

The rufous whistler is also known as the mock whipbird or thunderbird due to its explosive song. It is found throughout most of Australia in areas with tracts of open forest through to urban areas where there are plenty of trees and shrubs. It has a rather large, rounded head and robust bill.

DESCRIPTION: The male has mid-grey upper parts with duskier wings. Black encircles a white throat and passes through ruby eyes, while the breast is rufous, merging to grey on the upper flanks. The females generally have brownish-grey upper parts and faint streaking on the head, throat and upper breast. The birds are about 17 centimetres long.

STATUS AND DISTRIBUTION: The rufous whistler is common throughout its range, either resident or nomadic in WA. It also lives on many coastal islands.

PREFERRED HABITAT: This bird favours open forests, woodlands, scrubby areas, from coasts to mallee and mulga scrublands in arid inland areas. It is absent from the taller, denser forests.

LIFE HISTORY: Whistlers take their food, mostly insects and grubs, while methodically scrutinising foliage, often flying to seize prey from leaves. Fruit and berries are sometimes taken. Pairs establish boundaries during the breeding season which are defended by song and vigorous dance. Courtship displays involve bowing, bobbing and the spreading of wings.

CALL: While the call is a succession of musical chattering, the song, especially in breeding season, is a loud tuneful "pee-pee-pee, joey-joey-joey", ending with an "eeee-chong".

Male rufous whistler with chicks

Photo – Norman Chaffer Estate/Nature Focus

LITTLE WATTLEBIRD

(Anthochaera chrysoptera)

The little wattlebird is from one of Australia's most widespread and well differentiated families of birds. The great divergence seen in the honeyeaters is brought about by the abundance and dominance of the eucalypts, grevilleas, banksias, acacias and other nectar and insect-bearing flowering trees.

DESCRIPTION: The little wattlebird is similar to the larger red wattlebird but has a finer build. It reaches some 30 centimetres long and has a tapered tail. It is a brownish-grey colour, with fine white droplet-shaped streaks on its back and underparts. The crown and mantle are plain, while the lower sides of the face have a white sash. White tufts are also evident at the sides of the breast. Males and females look similar, but the male is distinctly larger.

OTHER NAMES: Western wattlebird, lunulated wattlebird.

STATUS AND DISTRIBUTION: This bird is common in the coastal regions and nearby ranges of south-western WA.

PREFERRED HABITAT: It lives in flowering woodlands, shrublands, forests and gardens.

LIFE HISTORY: The little wattlebird is found mostly in small colonies, spaced between the groups of flowering trees and shrubs. Most of its energy is obtained from nectar, but insects and spiders are also consumed. The young are fed mainly insects, as they need protein to grow. One chick is usually raised in a territory that is vigorously defended.

CALL: The call while feeding is a cheeping weep, similar to the immature birds. Occasionally a loud "chaawk" or "chock" by the male or high twittering by the female, are used to mark territory. The songs are usually followed by bill snapping, with clattering "chocks" and bubbling by the male.

WHITE-NAPED HONEYEATER
(Melithreptus lunatus)

The white-naped honeyeater is an active bird, foraging vigorously through foliage and blossom or darting skywards to take insects on the wing. Like other honeyeaters, its brush-like tongue is adept at extracting nectar from flowers.

DESCRIPTION: The bird has a small, neat appearance and the male and female are similar in colour and size. The crown and nape are black, with a thin white band around the nape stopping short of the eyes. The upper parts of the bird are olive green and the underparts white. A crescent of skin over the eye is white.

STATUS AND DISTRIBUTION: The white-naped honeyeater is common throughout the forests of south-western Australia and occurs in eastern Australia, from Adelaide to the Atherton Tableland in Queensland, and up to a few hundred kilometres inland. The western birds are slightly larger.

PREFERRED HABITAT: These birds inhabit the canopy of eucalypt forests.

LIFE HISTORY: The white-naped honeyeater lives in pairs and small communal groups. It will forage through outer branches and foliage, at times hanging upside down searching for insects and probing blossoms. Other members of the group help the senior breeding pair to feed and raise nestlings. Each nest is a delicate, deep cup of fine grass, bark and cobwebs. It is defended with vigour and aggression.

CALL: The call is a liquid mellow "tsew-tsew-tsew" and a harsh grating "sherp-sherp", which is often repeated. A soft but tense "pew-pew-pew" is sounded as an alarm call when a predator is detected.

MISTLETOEBIRD

(Dicaeum hirundinaceum)

Mistletoebirds are common, particularly around fruiting mistletoes. Although small and unobtrusive, they draw attention to themselves with short, sharp calls. When a mistletoebird squeezes a ripe berry in its bill the skin splits, popping out the sugar-coated seed. The bird swallows the seed, leaving the empty skin on the plant. The nutritious part of the pulp is rapidly digested, but the sticky inner layer remains intact, ready to glue the seed to a branch when it passes through the bird. A bird will often sit lengthways on a branch to excrete and even wipe its bottom on it, conveniently attaching the seed to it, where it will later germinate.

DESCRIPTION: Mistletoebirds are tiny, no more than 11 centimetres long. The males have a brilliant crimson breast; and their upper body is a glossy bluish-black. The breast and belly is white and grey with a central black streak. Females are much more subdued, with dull grey colouring.

STATUS AND DISTRIBUTION: The species is found throughout the Australian mainland.

PREFERRED HABITAT: They are quite nomadic and found almost anywhere with flowering mistletoes.

LIFE HISTORY: Mistletoebirds usually forage alone. They live almost exclusively on mistletoe berries but do take insects and other fruit from time to time. They breed from October to March. The nest is built by the female, who suspends it from a tree or branch. It is held together by cobwebs. There are typically three young and their heads and gaping beaks are quite a sight, as they emerge from the pouch-like nest to beg their parents for food.

CALL: They make a single high-pitched whistle in flight. The song is composed of two or three rising and falling whistled notes.

Above: *Female mistletoebird*   Below: *The male*

SPOTTED PARDALOTE

(Pardalotus punctatus)

The crown, wings and tail of this attractive little bird are decorated with numerous white spots. It excavates nesting burrows in low banks on the ground. These slope downwards and are up to one and a half metres deep.

DESCRIPTION: Spotted pardalotes have a black crown decorated with white spots, beneath which is a white brow. The face and neck is patterned with black, grey and white. The mid-back is brown to black, with attractive lighter markings, and the wing and tail feathers are black with white tips. The throat and undertail are a bright yellow and the breast and belly are pale yellow to white. These small birds only grow up to 10 centimetres long.

OTHER NAMES: Diamond bird, spotted diamond bird.

STATUS AND DISTRIBUTION: Spotted pardalotes are common across the southern and eastern coasts of Australia.

PREFERRED HABITAT: They favour eucalypt forests of any age, open woodlands and mallee areas, usually in higher rainfall zones.

LIFE HISTORY: Spotted pardalotes breed between August and January. They lay from three to six eggs in a loosely woven dome of grass and other fibre. Both parents cooperate to dig out the burrow, defend their breeding and foraging territory, incubate the eggs and feed the baby birds. They feed on lerps and other insects in the tree tops, making rapid mouse-like movements. Spotted pardalotes tend to be reasonably nomadic when not breeding and form wandering bands of between 10 and 100. These do not usually travel great distances.

CALL: While feeding, spotted pardalotes typically make a short series of mewing whistles to keep in contact.

STRIATED PARDALOTE
(Pardalotus striatus)

These active little birds pick at leaves and the outer twigs of eucalypt trees for bugs, lerps, ants, thrips and many other insects.

DESCRIPTION: They have a black crown that is usually streaked with white, and their black tail is quite stubby. The back is usually greyish-brown in colour and the black wings have a red or yellow spot at the tip of the shoulder. A thick stripe above the eye is bright yellow nearest the beak and then white, and the cream undersides also have a central yellow line that forks into each side of the breast.

STATUS AND DISTRIBUTION: Striated pardalotes are common and found throughout most of Australia.

PREFERRED HABITAT: The species favours open eucalypt forests and woodlands.

LIFE HISTORY: Southern populations may fly north or inland in autumn and winter. They breed between June and January in cup-shaped nests within the hollows of trees at least 10 metres high. The males become quite vocal with the onset of breeding. The breeding pair may be assisted by other family members.

CALL: Striated pardalotes call to each other by means of soft repeated trills. The song is loud, fast and repeated rapidly.

SIGHTING RECORD

SPECIES	DATE	LOCALITY	REMARKS
emu			
brown goshawk			
wedge-tailed eagle			
red-tailed black-cockatoo			
Baudin's black-cockatoo			
purple-crowned lorikeet			
red-capped parrot			
western rosella			
pallid cuckoo			
tawny frogmouth			
scarlet robin			
white-breasted robin			
western yellow robin			
golden whistler			
grey fantail			

Red-tailed black-cockatoo

SIGHTING RECORD

SPECIES	DATE	LOCALITY	REMARKS
splendid fairy-wren			
red-winged fairy-wren			
white-browed scrubwren			
western gerygone			
inland thornbill			
western thornbill			
yellow-rumped thornbill			
varied sittella			
rufous whistler			
little wattlebird			
white-naped honeyeater			
mistletoebird			
spotted pardalote			
striated pardalote			

Tawny frogmouth

INDEX